Stoic Productivity

Maximize Your Efficiency in a Distracted World

Table of Contents

Chapter 1. Introduction

Delve into a world where your productivity scales new heights, unswayed by the storms of external distractions in our Special Report titled "Stoic Productivity: Maximize Your Efficiency in a Distracted World." Our exciting report is a superb blend of ancient stoic philosophy and modern productivity strategies that empower you to take control of your day, accomplish tasks effectively, and consistently succeed amidst the inevitable hustle-bustle of contemporary life. Packaged with simple yet powerful techniques and inspiring real-world examples, it's crafted to inspire, motivate, and equip you for the journey you are about to embark upon. Remember, it's not just a report, it's an invitation to experience a transformative stoic way of life that leads to enhanced efficiency. Your gateway to unmatched productivity begins right here, right now; the world may be a chaotic dance of distractions, but you, fueled by Stoic Productivity, can be the eye of that storm, calm and composed!

Chapter 2. Understanding Stoicism and Productivity

Stoicism, a philosophical school originating from ancient Greece, offers fundamental tools for enhancing productivity while maintaining sanity in the bustling chaos of the modern world. It focuses on distinguishing what's within our control from the events outside our purview, allowing us to steer our concentration and effort exclusively towards the formers. It espouses the practice of virtue as the highest form of happiness while teaching us to accept life's trials, encouraging a robust resilience to external circumstances.

Chapter 3. Stoicism: An Overview

As one discovers Stoicism, it's crucial to grasp its roots — tracing back to circa 300 BC in Athens, Greece. Zeno of Citium, a merchant turned philosopher, established the Stoic school of thought, later augmented by philosophers like Seneca, Marcus Aurelius, and Epictetus. Stoic wisdom is encapsulated in their texts, influencing people centuries later and illuminating paths towards serenity, wisdom, and inner peace.

Stoicism is grounded on four cardinal virtues: Wisdom (or Prudence), Courage, Justice, and Temperance (or Moderation). These underline the stoic approach to life:

1. Wisdom: Understanding how to act and feel appropriately. It depicts the strength in judgment, enabling us to make right decisions.

2. Courage: The audacity to confront challenges, pain, and adversities.

3. Justice: treating all individuals fairly, ensuring we do no harm, and helping others when possible.

4. Temperance: Moderation or self-restraint in all aspects of life, balancing desires and needs keeping long-term goals in mind.

Learning to identify and practicing these virtues can significantly improve our productivity, personal well-being, and interpersonal relationships.

Chapter 4. Stoicism and Its Control Dichotomy

An essential Stoic concept is the Dichotomy of Control, a powerful mental model distinguishing things within our purview from the uncontrollable events. Epictetus, in his "Enchiridion," emphasizes things within our control (our beliefs, judgments, desires, and actions) and things that we don't govern (what other people think or do, the weather, the past or future events). Understanding this dichotomy and focusing energy solely on areas within our control can reduce anxiety, stress, and frustration while promoting productivity gains.

Chapter 5. Productivity: A Contemporary Challenge

Productivity challenges weren't as acute centuries ago as they are in today's fast-paced, distraction-filled world. With the advent of hyper-connectivity, the average person is bombarded by an overwhelming amount of information, diverting attention from the task at hand. Maximizing productivity, thus, is paramount, and calls for strategies to manage time, priorities, and energy efficiently.

Modern interpretations of productivity focus on achieving more in less time. Yet, a healthier and more sustainable definition prioritizes the quality of work over quantity, aiming for optimum results with minimum wasted effort.

Chapter 6. Marrying Stoicism and Productivity

Bridging Stoicism and productivity synthesizes a powerful approach to life and work. Stoic philosophy endorses mindfulness, meaningful work, and a strong sense of purpose, therefore acting as a natural ally to productivity.

Stoicism invokes the practice of setting clear goals and doing our best to achieve them while remaining detached from the results. The Stoic Productivity system inspires us to concentrate on the journey more than the destination, appreciating each achievement while recognizing the inherent learning in failures. Productivity, similarly, values task completion without being obsessed with the outcomes.

Strategic practices like time-blocking, removal of distractions, monotasking, and frequent self-reflection are all rooted in Stoic wisdom, thereby improving our productivity. Furthermore, it steers us clear from the trap of busyness without productivity, helping us prioritize effectively and work towards our goals despite potential chaos.

Stoicism also encourages us to constantly question our values, motives and actions. This introspection can lead to the elimination of wasteful tasks, boosting productivity by aligning our actions with our higher purpose.

Chapter 7. Stoic Productivity Strategy: A Practical Guide

Applying Stoic principles to our lives can revolutionize our productivity.

1. Take the long view: Remember mortal nature and the insignificance of single events in the grand scheme of life.

2. Accept the inevitable: Prepare for adversity and handle it with grace and wisdom.

3. Dichotomy of Control: Recognize what's within your power and what isn't to focus your energy wisely.

4. Mindfulness: Consciously device strategies to maintain awareness and focus on tasks.

5. Seek virtue: Make decisions guided by the Stoic cardinal virtues.

Adopting these principles requires sincere commitment and practice, but the rewards – a life well-lived, marked by wisdom, resilience, fulfillment, inner peace, and productivity - is within your grasp. As Seneca reminds us, "Luck is what happens when preparation meets opportunity." Brace yourself for the stoic journey to enhanced productivity!

Chapter 8. Embracing Chaos: Cultivating an Unshakeable Mindset

Train stations come alive during rush hours. The continuous inflow and outflow of people can overwhelm anyone not used to the ruckus. But take a closer look. Amidst this commotion, you will find an efficient system at work. People moving with purpose and certainty in a setting that may otherwise seem chaotic at the first glance. Such an observation is a fitting analogy for a stoic's mindset vis-à-vis life's numerous distractions.

8.1. An Introspective Journey

Understanding this philosophy requires us to begin by introspecting and understanding our habits, reactions, and impulses. We humans are often trapped in a cycle of reaction, spurred by stimuli that arise in our environment. This cycle tends to limit our perception of control, making us creatures of circumstance rather than masters of our destinies.

Stoicism, however, proposes an entirely different approach to life. In situations where the noise of external stimuli reaches a crescendo, stoicism teaches us to listen to the silence within, to disengage from the chaos without losing our place in it - a balance that allows us to maintain our productive stride, unscathed by the turmoil around us.

8.2. Bucking the Reactive Trend

This may seem implausible or even impossible, but the beauty of stoicism lies in its simplicity. Stoicism isn't about resisting or denying external distractions but rather about redefining our relationship with them.

We spend a significant portion of our lives reacting. An unpleasant email could ruin our mood; unforeseen traffic could spike our stress levels; a random social media post could spark a spiral of negative thoughts. Stoicism prompts us to question - why should our inner peace be susceptible to such trivialities?

A stoic mindset encourages us to step back and evaluate whether the circumstances warrant the level of emotional energy we often expend in our reactionary mode. Stoicism doesn't dismiss emotions. Instead, it promotes a more thoughtful response, where emotions serve us instead of guiding us. By refusing to be led by sporadic emotional upheavals, we become more resilient - a trait that directly enhances our productivity by keeping us focused and grounded, despite distractions.

8.3. A Paradigm shift

This new approach of perceiving the world might feel foreign, but remember that every transformative journey begins with a single step. This step is the recognition of the dichotomy of control, which is a fundamental principle in stoic philosophy. It encourages us to differentiate between things within our control and those that are not.

The only things truly within our control are our actions, thoughts, and responses. Recognizing this simple truth can help us tune out the multitude of distractions which do not directly impact these aspects under our control.

8.4. Stoic Mindset in Action

To cultivate a stoic mindset, begin with reflecting on your reactions when faced with distractions. Be conscious of your emotional shifts, mindfulness of which will lead you to identify patterns. Are you easily swayed by criticism? Do unexpected challenges make you anxious?

Next, consider how you can mitigate these reactions. Perhaps you have a meeting that consistently triggers stress. Instead of approaching it with dread, envision it as an opportunity to test your resilience. Adopt the mantra 'this too shall pass,' thereby adopting an emotional equilibrium.

8.5. Stoic Tools for Productivity

Implementing the stoic philosophy to augment productivity involves realigning your focus onto what truly matters. The serenity prayer, famously associated with stoicism, is a powerful tool in this regard: "Grant me the serenity to accept the things I cannot change, the courage to change the things I can, and the wisdom to know the difference."

Another efficient stoic tool is negative visualization. This practice allows you to premeditate on potential distractions or obstacles and devise ways to deal with them. By preparing for them mentally, you are not caught off guard when they occur, ensuring your productivity remains unfazed.

8.6. Embracing the Storm

Just like the train station, life, with all its complexity, can be overwhelming. Cultivating a stoic mindset is akin to finding tranquility amidst this seeming chaos. It is a quiet assertion of control - not over the world or circumstances, but over oneself.

Although it's important to realize that adapting to a stoic way of life doesn't mean the absence of distractions. Instead, it means changing our perception and reaction to those distractions. It's not so much about the suppression of emotional reaction as it is about the mastery of it.

Remember, like all good things, cultivating a stoic mindset requires practice. Start small, take one potential distraction at a time, and implement stoic techniques to navigate around them effectively.

While the distraction-laden world continues its chaotic dance, you will discover that you have become the eye of that storm - a zone characterized by controlled emotions, thoughtful responses, and sustained productivity. And thus, you will have successfully embraced chaos, with a resilient and unshakeable stoic mindset.

Chapter 9. Digging Deep into Stoic Values: Virtue, Wisdom, Fortitude, and Temperance

In the realm of Stoicism, virtue is not merely an abstract concept but a realizable aspiration, integral for achieving an equanimous state of mind and maximizing productivity. It's compelling to note that Stoicism doesn't categorize virtue into singular standalone qualities; rather, it envelops a cluster of cardinal virtues, namely – wisdom, fortitude, and temperance.

9.1. The Cardinal Virtue: Wisdom

Wisdom, in Stoicism, is not just the accumulation of knowledge but the discernment to act impeccably during decision-making processes. It's predicated on the comprehension of the natural world and the human role within it, enabling one to make responsible choices, unscathed by ephemeral emotions. Wisdom is thus the remedy to impulsivity caused by external stimuli that often hinder productivity.

Further, wisdom aids in distinguishing between what is in our control and what is not – a fundamental tenet of Stoicism. This clarity carves out space for focus on what truly matters, aiding in effective task prioritization and efficient time management, correspondingly boosting productivity.

The implementation of Stoic wisdom can transform usual responses into thoughtful actions. It thus stimulates intelligent decisions, ensuring we are acting out of reason, not out of fleeting emotions or external pressures. This capability is extraordinarily valuable in a modern context, where we must navigate an elaborate network of tasks, responsibilities, and expectations.

9.2. Fostering Fortitude: The Stoic Resilience

Fortitude holds a treasured place within Stoic virtues, often portrayed as indomitable resilience or morale when faced with adversity. It's a quality that empowers one to endure difficult situations with courage, showcasing their inner strength of character.

Fortitude makes us resilient to external distractions, providing robustness to the mind and allowing us to concentrate on our work despite surrounding chaos. In this light, fortitude builds the foundation for productivity. The coupling of wisdom and fortitude allows us to effectively navigate the intricacies of complex scenarios and maintain our workflow, irrespective of external disturbances.

On days when it seems impossible to move beyond discomfort, when where we wish to be seems lightyears away from the reality we experience, fortitude guides us through. It enables us to endure, persist and push forward, leading us to the realm of progress, one step at a time.

9.3. Mastering Temperance: Prudent Moderation

Temperance, a paramount virtue in Stoicism, bears insight into prudent moderation. It's not about extinguishing our desires or passions, rather, it's about controlling them, ensuring they don't overpower our reason, subsequently preventing us from swaying away from our goals.

Mastery over one's desires and passions directly propels towards productivity. It ensures our actions are driven from an internal locus of control and propels us towards the consummation of tasks that align with our long-term objectives.

Temperance promotes balance, a critical aspect of sound mind space, which consequently bolsters concentration and focus towards the task at hand. It also prevents the exhaustion of mental resources due to over indulgence, ensuring that we remain steady on our path towards goal attainment.

In a world brimming with distractions and stimuli, the practice of temperance can create a personal sanctuary of focus. It assists in warding off the incessant demands of immediate gratification and propels us towards the path of long-term success.

9.4. Virtue: The Stoic Key to Productivity

The Stoics believed that these virtues - wisdom, fortitude, and temperance, acted as guiding principles for a tranquil life. By incorporating these timeless values into daily routines and decision-making processes, they provide a robust framework for enhancing productivity.

Understanding and living these Stoic virtues empower us to counter life's challenges with equanimity and control. They equip us with tools to remain unswayed in the face of distractions, keeping our focus on what is truly important - achieving our goals and realizing our vision.

The journey towards productivity, as mirrored through the lens of Stoicism, is not about relentless pursuit, but purposeful progress. It's about nurturing the right virtues, cultivating a resilient mindset, and steadfastly sailing the ship of life amidst the tumultuous storm of distractions, fuelled by the relentless engine of virtue-driven productivity!

Chapter 10. The Wisdom of Seneca, Epictetus, and Marcus Aurelius: Key Productivity Lessons

The wise teachings of the Stoics, including Seneca, Epictetus, and Marcus Aurelius, entail powerful lessons on productivity, resilience, and focus. Unpacking and applying these lessons in our contemporary world can result in extraordinary enhancement in our ability to manage distractions and accomplish our intended tasks more efficiently.

10.1. Embracing the Dichotomy of Control

The heart of Stoic teaching lies in distinguishing the things within our control from those which are beyond it. This dichotomy of control is key to productivity. Epictetus, a slave turned philosopher, asserts that our thoughts, opinions, desires, and sensations are within our control. External things like fame, health, wealth are not in our realm of control.

Understanding and accepting this dichotomy can empower us to channel our time, energy, and resources towards the tasks under our control. Uncertain outcomes and distractions fueled by external elements will thus become secondary, bringing out the best of our efficiency.

10.2. Negative Visualization and Anticipatory Thinking

A characteristic Stoic practice articulated by Seneca, 'Negative Visualization' or 'Premeditatio Malorum' (the pre-meditation of evils), involves anticipating adversities and obstacles that may confront us. Rather than promoting pessimism, this practice aids in preparing ourselves for potential difficulties, leading to better management of such situations when they actually occur.

For increased productivity, we could apply this principle by visualizing the potential hindrances likely to interrupt our work flow, and strategizing ways to mitigate those disruptors beforehand. This preemptive thinking can lead to smoother, more focused productivity sessions.

10.3. Parallels Between Nature and Productivity

Marcus Aurelius, a Roman Emperor and renowned Stoic philosopher, relied heavily on analogies from nature to illustrate life lessons. His 'Meditations' implies that all things in nature are interconnected in a larger scheme and we have to play our part responsibly.

This analogy can be taken to our professional and personal life. Each of our tasks, regardless of how insignificant they may appear, play a crucial role in our overall productivity. Recognizing this interconnectedness can help us ensure dedicated focus on every task we undertake.

10.4. Seneca's Lessons on Timeliness

Seneca wisely stated that, 'It is not that we have a short time to live, but that we waste much of it'. He asserted the need for allocating time judiciously, just as we do with money and other resources.

In terms of productivity, understanding the importance of time management is paramount. Prioritizing tasks, setting deadlines, tracking time spent on each task, and adequate planning can help us reduce time wasting, resulting in noticeable improvement in productivity.

10.5. Epictetus on Acceptance and Adaptability

Epictetus emphasized on accepting things as they are and adapting to circumstances. He exhorted that we should not expect the world to adapt according to our convenience, rather we should modify ourselves to suit the external environment.

Applying this lesson to our work-life means being flexible with changes, and having the resilience to adjust to changing work demands, work hours, project scopes, and team dynamics. It involves maintaining our productivity levels despite experiencing changing circumstances, inevitably enhancing our efficiency.

10.6. Marcus Aurelius on 'Willed Actions'

Marcus Aurelius considered 'Just that which is happening and just that which is unfolding now' calling these as 'Willed Actions.' The principle implies focusing on the immediate task at hand.

In terms of productivity, this concept can be applied by practicing mindfulness and working on one task at a time, fully present and engaged. This can not only enhance the quality of the work, but also reduce the time consumed in switching between various tasks, thereby boosting productivity.

Implementing these ancient wisdoms may not be an easy transition, and it never promises instant results. However, over time, their transformative power will become evident as we gain control over our distractions and enhance our productivity. Inspired by the Stoics, we would do well to remember that storms of distractions may rise and fall, but we can remain unswayed – much like a lighthouse amidst the waves – focused, productive, and propelled towards our goals.

Chapter 11. Mindfulness and Stoic Productivity: The Perfect Synergy

There's a certain simplicity in the beauty of mindfulness. It's the gentle wave that washes over the shores of chaos, bringing tranquility. Combine this powerful calming force with the practicality of Stoic philosophy, and we have a match made in productivity heaven. Both mindfulness and Stoicism revolve around self-control, self-awareness, and living in the present—values that have immense implications for enhancing productivity.

11.1. The Roots of Mindfulness and Stoicism

Mindfulness, with its roots in Buddhist philosophy, encourages us to wholly focus on the present moment, gently acknowledging and accepting our feelings, thoughts, and sensations. One of the main goals of mindfulness is to quieten the mind, creating space for focus and creativity, and tackling one task at a time with full awareness.

Similarly, Stoicism, an ancient Greek philosophy, teaches us to differentiate between things we can control and those we can't, urging us to focus our energy on the former. It implores acceptance of external events as they are, understanding that our reactions are within our control.

Indeed, both doctrines preach acceptance and control over our mind, creating a fertile ground for an unprecedented level of productivity to flourish.

11.2. Applying Mindfulness to Productivity

Now, why should mindfulness matter to people wanting to be more productive? The answer is simple: being thoroughly present.

Mindfulness disrupts the cycle of knee-jerk reactions to endless notifications, impulsive task-switching, and the constant rush to do more, faster. By training you to focus your attention on the present task, mindfulness makes room for deeper concentration, creativity, and measured decision-making. You stop being a puppet, yanked by the strings of distractions, and become the calm, composed master of your activities. It's, therefore, unsurprising that companies like Google and Apple utilize mindfulness techniques to improve their employees' productivity.

11.3. Techniques for a Mindful Stoic

Practice mindfulness through simple routines. Start by dedicating a few moments in your day to sit quietly, allowing your thoughts to flow without judgment. Observe each thought as it arises and passes, helping your mind to settle into the present moment. Regular meditation practice, coupled with conscious attempts to remain mindful during everyday tasks, can gradually improve your attention span and focus.

Stoicism is all about understanding and working within your locus of control. Keep a journal for self-reflection, write down instances where you felt controlled by external influences, and make a conscious effort to alter your reactions. Marcus Aurelius, the Roman Emperor and a prominent Stoic philosopher, was known for his journaling habit, which helped him maintain calm and composed demeanor amid the chaos of ruling a vast empire.

11.4. The Intersection of Mindfulness and Stoicism

While mindfulness improves your focus, the tenets of Stoicism—like the dichotomy of control and the acceptance of change—are inherently stress-reducing, further boosting your productivity. By accepting situations as they are and focusing on your response instead of the circumstance, you reduce the mental exhaustion associated with stress, frustration, or anger, leaving more energy to direct towards productive tasks.

Moreover, the Stoic emphasis on virtue aligns with being mindful of our actions. Consider the wise words of Epictetus, "It's not what happens to you, but how you react that matters." You might not control the arrival of an unexpected email, just as you can't stop a distracting thought from arising during meditation. But your attitude towards it—whether to immediately respond to the email or bring your focus back to your task, or gently acknowledge the disrupting thought and return to your meditative state—determines your efficiency.

11.5. The Power Pack: Mindful Stoic Productivity

The blend of mindfulness and Stoic philosophy provides a powerful productivity formula referred to as 'Mindful Stoic Productivity.' Mindfulness teaches us to stay anchored in the present—and that's also where our productivity lies. While Stoicism, by helping us decipher what's within our control, lays bare the areas deserving our attention and energy. Combining these forces, we create a robust, self-aware, resilient, and more productive self.

Mindful Stoic Productivity isn't just a strategy; it's a way of life. It empowers you to create a productivity system that depends not on external structures but on your internal capability to manage thoughts and regulate emotions. By keeping your mind at the center of your productivity journey, it ensures that your efficiency isn't swayed by the storms of distraction around you.+

In the end, both mindfulness and Stoicism aim to build a life characterized by calm and serenity—a life where you respond rather than react. The application of these principles to productivity might well be the remedy for the relentless hustle and exhaustion epidemic prevalent in the modern world. You might find the perfect synergy of mindfulness and Stoic productivity being a beacon, guiding you to a state of efficient tranquility amidst the chaotic dance of distractions. Indeed, what an invincible alliance they form!

Chapter 12. Stoic Dichotomy of Control: Mastering What's in Your Hand

Beyond the foreground of the mind lies a core principle of stoic philosophy often disguised by its apparent simplicity - 'The Dichotomy of Control.' Challenging to master, but once understood and freely embraced, it can radically redefine our interaction with the world. Life, in essence, tosses at us a mix of parts we can control and parts we cannot. This dichotomy, rather than a source of despair, offers grounds for empowerment.

12.1. Understanding the Dichotomy of Control

Stoic philosopher Epictetus imperatively stated that "some things are in our control and others not." Here we must differentiate between what constitutes the former and the latter in our lives - a primal step in our journey towards stoic productivity.

So what are the things within our control? Typically, these are our thoughts, beliefs, perceptions, and actions - the internal elements whose sole master is our own self. They can be instigated, altered, and extinguished at the will of our minds; no external force holds the reign.

On the contrary, the weather, your flight's delay, or even the world economy - factors that remain beyond our reach directly or indirectly are not within our control. How often do we let these externalities dictate our mood or cripple our progress? Refrain from this unnecessary mental strain by acknowledging that these externalities do not warrant our worry or distress.

The dichotomy of control aims to sharpen the focus towards internal elements and mitigate the undue influence of external factors on our quality of life and productivity levels.

12.2. Implementing the Dichotomy of Control

Abstracting from the wisdom of stoicism, we need to modify our responses to different life situations. Let's explore how to implement this concept in our daily living and work scenarios.

Consider a project deadline that looms ahead, seemingly insurmountable. The dichotomy of control suggests first segregating elements within and beyond your command.

Things within your control include the effort you put in, your strategy to tackle the tasks, and your mental attitude towards the assignment. Elements beyond your control may involve sudden technical glitches, team members falling ill, or last-minute alterations from stakeholders.

React to situations within your control with meticulous planning, appropriate action, and assertive follow-up. But for factors beyond your control, shift your approach by accepting the occurrence and adapting to the changed landscape.

This strategic approach paints an alternative outlook towards potential stressors. It allows you to conserve the energy habitually expended on worrying about the uncontrollable and directs it towards productive channels that you can influence.

12.3. Benefits of Mastering the Dichotomy of Control

By leveraging the dichotomy of control, you can profoundly transform your productivity. Let's explore some key benefits:

1. Reduced Stress: By distinguishing what's in your control and letting go of what's not, you eliminate a significant source of stress. That way, you can dedicate your mental power to things that you can genuinely influence.

2. Greater Focus: Recognizing your circle of control brings about a greater focus on things that matter, blurring the distractions outside the circle.

3. Enhanced Decision Making: It allows you to make sound decisions, as you're aware of your capacities and limitations.

4. Increased Adaptability: The dichotomy of control builds a resilience mechanism that enables you to adapt to unexpected situations, thus boosting your capability to bounce back from setbacks.

5. Amplified Productivity: Ultimately, reduced stress, enhanced focus, and adaptability catapult your productivity to higher levels.

12.4. Harnessing the Power of the Dichotomy of Control for Enhanced Productivity

Anchoring on the philosophy of the Dichotomy of Control not only benefits our holistic wellbeing but also contributes significantly towards bolstering efficiency and productivity.

Contemplate on this stoic principle and incorporate it into your thought process and actions. Wielding this tool in your productivity arsenal encourages you to discern and impact areas you can control and develop an active coping mechanism for the rest, thereby preempting futile stressors and maximizing the outcome of your efforts.

Productivity, in this stoic context, transforms from being a summoning act of willpower, to a consequence of wisdom, understanding, and disciplined application of the dichotomy of control. Embrace this stoic principle and navigate smoothly through the ebbs and flows of life while scaling new heights of productivity and efficient execution. The harmony of dichotomy of control and productivity creates what we call 'Stoic Productivity.'

In summary, navigating the distracted world with the navigator of the stoic principle of dichotomy of control ensures your vessel stays on course, regardless of how tumultuous the sea of life becomes. Employ this principle, epitomize stoic productivity, and shape your unique trajectory of effectiveness and potency.

Let the Dichotomy of Control be your compass in the voyage of life, helping you conquer every storm with calmness, grit, and unprecedented productivity. Remember, the distractions may be unruly, yet you, with stoic productivity as your shield, can remain the calm center, defying them all!

Chapter 13. Stoic Techniques to Overcome Distractions and Enhance Focus

In a world brimming with diversions, staying focused is no small feat. The Stoic philosophy offers profound techniques to mollify the intensity of modern distractions and heighten focus. These strategies, if prudently utilized, can bolster your attention span, enhance productivity, and create a path of ease even in the midst of a frenzy.

13.1. Understanding Distractions

To address the challenge of distractions, we must first understand them. Stoicism encourages a meeting of the inward and outward, asking us to explore the origin of our distractions before delving into overcoming them. Are these distractions external, such as the ding of a new email notification or the chatter around you? Or are they internal, like your incessant thoughts, worries, or daydreams? The key to addressing these distractions rests in comprehending their true nature, segregating them based on their source, and then applying techniques to counteract them effectively.

13.2. Countering External Distractions

External distractions are inherently unpredictable, often breaking our focus at inopportune moments. While we may not control the existence of these botherations, how we respond to them is entirely within our reach. Through the lenses of Stoicism, here's how you can tackle these interruptions.

13.2.1. Practice Dispassionate Observation

Dispassionate observation is a potent stoic tool for coping with external distractions. It involves impartially observing the distraction without allowing it to stir your inner peace. For instance, rather than feeling irritated by the noise around you, acknowledge the sound as just another sensory input - neither positive nor negative.

13.2.2. Create a Conducive Environment

Design an environment that is conducive to focused work, limiting as many distractions as possible. A well-structured workspace can go a long way towards reducing the interference caused by external factors.

13.2.3. Embrace Preemptive Planning

Stoics are adept at employing forethought. Plan out tasks in advance, aiming to minimize the potential interruptions that could crop up. By predicting potential distractions, you can equip yourself to handle them more effectively.

13.3. Tackling Internal Distractions

Stoic philosophy can also offer valuable wisdom to handle internal distractions, which might evade detection but subtly eat away at your productivity.

13.3.1. Cultivate Self-awareness - The Bedrock of Stoicism

A key practice in Stoicism is the cultivation of self-awareness. It's a process of introspection that involves understanding the workings of your own mind. Exploring your thought patterns and acknowledging the inner disturbances that lead to distraction can provide you with greater control over your responses.

13.3.2. Practice Mindfulness

The practice of mindfulness is closely linked to the Stoic practice of self-awareness. By living in the present and focusing on your ongoing task, you halt the internal chatter and concentrate better. This process is aided by taking deliberate breathing pauses, fostering a sense of calm and clarity in your workflow.

13.3.3. Gedankenexperiment: The Stoic 'Thought Experiment'

Stoics utilized thought experiments for personal development and to mitigate distractions. This practice involves visualizing your activities and their potential outcomes. If you feel your mind drifting off into distractions, reorient it towards a productive thought experiment.

13.4. Synergizing the Techniques

While individual techniques are instrumental in overcoming distractions, their true power shines through when used synergistically. This involves tailoring a combination of techniques that best suits your distinct personal and professional situations. It means alternating between dispassionate observation and thought experiments, or using mindfulness during preemptive planning. The beauty of these stoic techniques is in their malleability - they can be honed and applied based on contextual nuances.

13.5. Conclusion: The Stoic Way to Overcome Distractions

The essence of overcoming distractions, as taught by the Stoics, lies in a blend of understanding, acceptance, and strategic action. It's about acknowledging distractions without giving them the power to disrupt. It's devising a plan of action without forgetting the forces that guide our lives are often beyond our control. Adopting this stoic perspective empowers you not only to tear down the barriers erected by distractions but also to build an environment – internal and external – conducive to deep, focused work.

Stoic techniques are not just theoretical constructs. When brought to life through consistent practice, they provide an effective framework for less distraction and more focus, equipping you with a skillset that elevates productivity and efficiency amidst the chaos of the external world.

Chapter 14. From Theory to Action: Practical Steps to Implement Stoic Productivity

Just how does one begin on a path to Stoic Productivity, applying an age-old philosophy into the demands of a technological, fast-paced modern lifestyle? Here, we lay out practical steps of how you can apply the principles of stoicism into your daily routine, making a smooth transition from theory to action.

14.1. Understand and Acknowledge Your Sphere of Control

Marcus Aurelius once stated, "You have power over your mind – not outside events. Realize this, and you will find strength." This is the first step on the path of Stoic Productivity: to delineate your outside events from your psychological responses towards them, to understand that the former may be out of your control, but the latter is completely within your power.

List various aspects of your life on a piece of paper, categorizing them into two sections: under your control and outside of your control. Most of your activities lie in the former, while the reactions of others, the weather, and global economic conditions, lie in the latter. The key is to focus your energies. Concentrate on what you can control, and detach from the uncontrollable aspects of life.

14.2. Simplify Your Life

"Keep busy with survival. Imitate the trees. Learn to lose in order to recover, and remember that nothing stays the same for long." These powerful words from the stoic philosopher, Seneca, remind us that life at its core is quite simple, and the key to productivity is unburdening ourselves from complexities.

In a technological world, distractions come hand-in-hand with convenience. Journey into digital minimalism: filter out unnecessary notifications, set aside dedicated hours where you use no devices, restrict the number of tabs open on your browser. Simplify your physical space: a clutter-free workspace makes a productive one. And above all, prioritize your own well-being, both mentally and physically, as it's the essence of stoic lifestyle.

14.3. Cultivate Emotional Resilience

A fundamental tenet of Stoicism is emotional resilience. Stoics strive to maintain a level-headedness regardless of external events. They acknowledge their emotions but don't let them master their decisions or productivity.

Implement mindfulness techniques to recognize your emotions when they emerge and to step back from them rather than react impulsively. Regular meditation is an effective practice that leads to better emotional regulation. Additionally, consider journaling to take note of and analyze your emotional patterns, turning your introspection into actionable insights, leading to growing emotional resilience.

14.4. Focus on Process over Outcome

Another crucial stoic teaching is focusing on the process rather than the outcome. Stoics believe that success lies not in the result but in the pursuit itself. This philosophy can be a game-changer when incorporated into your productivity strategies.

Refinery exercises such as task breakdown can help in this aspect. Dividing a large task into multiple 'mini-tasks' reduces feeling overwhelmed and offers numerous opportunities for small successes. In the end, you realize that the journey holds as much joy as the destination.

14.5. Mastery of Time

Ephemerality of time was a recurring theme in Stoic philosophy. Every moment is fleeting, never to return, making time our most precious resource. Understanding this concept is fundamental to mastering productivity.

Prioritize your tasks ruthily. Use time management techniques like time-blocking, where you allocate specific timeframes for specific activities, or the Pomodoro technique, where you work for a set amount of time then take short breaks. Practice mindfulness to remain present and maximize efficiency in the given task. All these methods are proven ways to achieve effective time utilization.

14.6. Daily Deliberate Practice

Lastly, remember that stoicism is a way of life, not an on-off switch. Stoic productivity isn't something that's achievable overnight. It's a journey rather than a destination. Daily practice is how this philosophy becomes a part of your core identity.

Start by beginning and ending each day with stoic reflection. Mornings can be reserved for evaluating your plan for the day, channelizing your energies, and setting a positive mental note. Evenings can be for introspection - reviewing your actions, identifying areas of improvement, and appreciating the growth. Over time, such dedicated practice will help you internalize stoicism, enhancing productivity and delivering a profound impact on your lifestyle.

Though this journey is individual and subjective, the steps provided here are broad and universally applicable. They beckon the initiation of a lifetime decision – a decision to choose calm, robustness, and efficiency over reactionary emotional responses, helping you lead a life of harmony and productivity. The world is indeed chaotic, but remember, you have the potential to be the calm center, to embrace Stoic Productivity. It's right here, right now – in the choices you make, the lifestyle you choose, and the path you decide to journey on. Take the plunge into a life of productive tranquility, a stoic life.

Chapter 15. Boosting Professional Life using Stoic Productivity

By harnessing the tenets of stoicism and integrating them with the modern productivity strategies, you can substantially boost your professional life. To facilitate a comprehensive understanding of leveraging stoic productivity, this chapter is divided into several subparts. Let's delve into the enthralling world of stoic productivity:

15.1. Combining Stoicism with Modern Professionalism

Stoicism, an ancient philosophy, lauds the importance of self-control, emotional resilience, and clear judgment. These are pivotal for professional life. In a contemporary corporate landscape marked by constant change, uncertainty, stress, and intense competition, stoicism offers an empowering framework for maintaining calmness and performing optimally.

Recognizing external elements beyond your control and focusing on personal efforts and reactions in managing professional duties can enhance productivity. For a stoic, every situation, no matter how seemingly adverse, is an opportunity to exercise virtues such as patience, courage, and persistence. By concentrating on actions within one's control and disregarding distractive external factors, you can significantly heighten professional productivity.

15.2. An Overview of Stoic Practices to Boost Professional Productivity

There are five main practices tied with Stoic productivity that can be used to increase your workplace efficiency. They are:

- Re-evaluating Perceptions and Judgments: Train your mind to interpret and respond to events at work more objectively.

- Dichotomy of Control: Learn to distinguish between what's within your control and what's not.

- Premeditatio Malorum: Practice advance reflection of potential setbacks, not in pessimism, but to bolster resilience.

- Practicing Virtue: Contribute upstanding professional behavior, leading to a positive workplace environment.

- Being Present: Foster mindful engagement in ongoing tasks, minimizing adverse impacts of past failures or future anxieties.

15.3. Re-evaluating Perceptions and Judgments

The first step towards stoic productivity is challenging your perceptions. The way you perceive a situation largely determines how you react or respond to it. Catastrophic thinking about an event, harsh judgments about colleagues, or unrealistic expectations about outcomes can thwart productivity. By challenging these unhelpful thought patterns and developing a more rational, objective view, you preserve mental energy and respond more effectively to situations at work.

For instance, consider a missed deadline. A non-stoic reaction might be panic, frustration, or self-criticism. Instead, a stoic approach encourages a more rational response: "Yes, I've missed this deadline, but I can learn from my mistakes and work on improving my time management." Being level-headed allows you to create practical strategies enhancing productivity.

15.4. Dichotomy of Control

The essence of stoic philosophy is understanding what one can control and what is beyond one's sphere of influence. Conventional productivity practices suggest exerting more control over one's environment. But Stoic productivity propounds a different approach — focusing on self-behavior, reactions, and efforts that are truly under our control while accepting immovable external conditions.

It implies you should direct your energy and efforts towards factors under your control: maintaining a disciplined lifestyle, nurturing positive relationships at work, acquiring new skills, and meeting project deadlines. On the other hand, factors you cannot control — such as company policies, market trends, or colleagues' behaviors — should not be those that unnecessarily drain your mental energy or detract from your focus.

15.5. Premeditatio Malorum

Premeditatio Malorum or premeditation of evils is another fundamental stoic practice. It involves contemplating possible future challenges or setbacks as part of your planning process. The goal is not to induce fear or worry, but to bolster your resilience and prepare for potential difficulties.

Incorporating this into your professional life, you might consider potential setbacks that could hurdle a project — maybe a team member falling sick, an unexpected budget cut, or necessary data being unavailable. These are not intended to discourage you, but to prompt proactive thinking and the preparation of contingency plans.

15.6. Practicing Virtue

Stoic philosophy emphasizes the importance of virtues such as wisdom, courage, justice, and temperance. The implementation of these virtues at the workplace can bolster a harmonious environment and cultivate a productive work ethic, contributing to heightened overall productivity.

By demonstrating wisdom, you can make judicious decisions, handle crises effectively, and guide your colleagues towards project goals. Courage allows you to voice your opinions, confront issues, and embrace new challenges. Justice ensures fair treatment of all team members and ethical handling of assignments. Temperance helps manage resources judiciously and promotes balance.

15.7. Being Present

Stoicism encourages mindfulness — being fully present in the current moment. This precludes the wastage of mental energy worrying about past mistakes or future concerns, channeling this energy into present tasks, therefore enhancing productivity.

Discard those worries over a past project failure that can't be rectified or the constant fretting over an upcoming presentation. Learn from past experiences, plan for the future, but stay immersed in the present task. This will not only enhance focus and productivity but also improve work quality.

With a blend of stoicism and modern productivity strategies, your professional life can witness tremendous growth. Remember, the key lies in maintaining emotional stability amidst chaos and focusing your efforts on attainable targets. As Seneca, the renowned Stoic philosopher, put it, "We suffer more in imagination than reality." By taking control of your thoughts and channeling your energy in the right direction, stoic productivity can become your strongest ally in overcoming the whirlwind of workplace challenges.

Chapter 16. Resilience and Adaptability: The Stoic Way for Sustained Efficiency

Resilience and adaptability form the very core of the stoic philosophy of life, defining one's ability to withstand adversity and bounce back from difficulties. The practice of stoicism enables one to maintain unbroken focus and deliver unwavering productivity, no matter what circumstances are at play.

16.1. Understanding Resilience and Adaptability

Before digging deeper into the Stoic approach to resilience and adaptability, let's begin by understanding the concepts themselves. Resilience is your ability to quickly recover from difficulties, challenges, or adversity. It's about bouncing back and persevering even when there are obstacles. On the other hand, adaptability is the capacity to adjust or be adjusted to new conditions or circumstances. In productivity terms, these are not merely desirable traits but essential tools for surviving and thriving in an increasingly competitive and fast-paced world.

16.2. The Underlying Premise of Stoic Philosophy

At the heart of stoicism lays the belief that while we may not have control over the events that occur in life, we can control how we interpret and react to them. This line of thought directly relates to our conversations about resilience and adaptability: being responsive, rather than reactive, to the world around us. Take, for example, the Serenity Prayer, which reverberates stoic wisdom: "God grant me the serenity to accept the things I cannot change, courage to change the things I can, and wisdom to know the difference."

16.3. Building Resilience: The Stoic Way

From a stoic perspective, the cultivation of resilience begins with an understanding and acceptance of the impermanence of things. Change, as they say, is the only constant. Stoicism impels adherents to learn to be content with what they have, to accept transient experiences with grace, and to resist the urge to excessively mourn losses or crave something more or different. Acceptance doesn't equal passivity or resignation, but a profound understanding that allows us to take constructive action without being held captive by situations.

16.4. Practicing Adaptability: Go With the Flow

Building on the resilience ingrained through stoic philosophy, adaptability emerges as a natural progression. It's not about resisting change, but harmonizing with it. Importantly, adaptability according to stoicism doesn't suggest indiscriminate flexibility, but to apply judgment and discretion along with it. When we adapt, we do so in accordance with our principles and values, ensuring that our productivity and actions always align with our higher objectives.

16.5. Stoic Practices to Boost Resilience and Adaptability

Several entries in Stoic literature provide practical advice and guidance on developing resilience and adaptability, serving as valuable tools for any modern professional or individual. Here are a few illustrative examples:

- Negative Visualization: This practice involves visualizing the worst-case scenarios. The goal of this technique is not pessimistic thinking, but the cultivation of gratitude for what you presently have and to mentally prepare for any potential setbacks.

- Voluntary Discomfort: Engaging in voluntary discomfort means intentionally undertaking challenging or uncomfortable tasks. The objective of this exercise is to grow accustomed to discomfort, build resilience, and develop a greater appreciation for simple comforts.

Build these practices into your everyday productivity habits, and observe these driving your workplace efficiency towards unparalleled heights, both in quality and quantity of output. Remember, the core of these ideas is to see the scenario for what it is – neither to brood over difficulties nor to ignore the challenges – but approach them with a proactive mentality of problem-solving.

Resilience and adaptability, as viewed from the Stoic lens, aren't mere strategies but a way of life. They prepare one to maximize efficiency not only during times of calm and routine, but more importantly, during periods of change, challenge, and uncertainty. As you explore and assimilate these lessons, remember that the journey to sustained productivity is not a one-time sprint, but a marathon requiring continuous learning, practice, and refinement.

In the essence of stoicism, view hurdles as opportunities, adapt to the circumstances with an open mind, maintain an unwavering focus on your goals, and propel your productivity from the ordinary to the extraordinary. You are the master of your actions and reactions. In a world inherently characterized by change and unpredictability, resilience and adaptability will be your steadfast allies in the quest for sustained efficiency. There's an incredible world waiting for you.

Charge forth with the power of Stoic Productivity and carve your path of excellence and accomplishment.